VIETNAMESE IN AMERICA

web enhanced at www.inamericabooks.com

LORI COLEMAN

LERNER PUBLICATIONS COMPANY / MINNEAPOLIS

Current information and statistics quickly become out of date. That's why we developed **www.inamericabooks.com**, a companion website to the **In America** series. The site offers lots of additional information—downloadable photos and maps and up-to-date facts through links to additional websites. Each link has been carefully selected by researchers at Lerner Publishing Group and is regularly reviewed and updated. However, Lerner Publishing Group is not responsible for the accuracy or suitability of material on websites that are not maintained directly by us. It is recommended that students using the Internet be supervised by a parent, a librarian, a teacher, or another adult.

Lerner Publications Company
A division of Lerner Publishing Group
241 First Avenue North
Minneapolis, MN 55401 U.S.A.

Website address: www.lernerbooks.com

Library of Congress Cataloging-in-Publication Data

Coleman, Lori.
    Vietnamese in America / by Lori Coleman.
        p.   cm. – (In America)
    Includes bibliographical references and index.
    ISBN: 0–8225–3951–9 (lib. bdg. : alk. paper)
    1. Vietnamese Americans—History—Juvenile literature. 2. Vietnamese Americans—Juvenile
literature. 3. Refugees—United States—Juvenile literature. [1. Vietnamese Americans.] I. Title.
II. Series: In America (Minneapolis, Minn.)
E184.V53C65 2005
973'.049592–dc22   2003023646

Manufactured in the United States of America
1 2 3 4 5 6 – JR – 10 09 08 07 06 05

CONTENTS

INTRODUCTION

In America, a walk down a city street can seem like a walk through many lands. Grocery stores sell international foods. Shops offer products from around the world. People strolling past may speak foreign languages. This unique blend of cultures is the result of America's history as a nation of immigrants.

Native peoples have lived in North America for centuries. The next settlers were the Vikings. In about A.D. 1000, they sailed from Scandinavia to lands that would become Canada, Greenland, and Iceland. In 1492 the Italian navigator Christopher Columbus landed in the Americas, and more European explorers arrived during the 1500s. In the 1600s, British settlers formed colonies that, after the Revolutionary War (1775–1783), would become the United States. And in the mid-1800s, a great wave of immigration brought millions of new arrivals to the young country.

Immigrants have many different reasons for leaving home. They may leave to escape poverty, war, or harsh governments. They may want better living conditions for themselves and their children. Throughout its history, America has been known as a nation that offers many opportunities. For this reason, many immigrants come to America.

Moving to a new country is not easy. It can mean making a long, difficult journey. It means leaving home and starting over in an unfamiliar place. But it also means using skill, talent, and determination to build a new life. The In America series tells the story of immigration to the United States and the search for fresh beginnings in a new country—in America.

VIETNAMESE IN AMERICA

Most people who came to the United States from Vietnam did so in the 1970s and 1980s. They fled during and after a terrible civil war that tore apart their homeland. Arriving as refugees, many came without possessions. Few could speak English.

Since coming to America, Vietnamese refugees have made great strides. They have become productive members of American society, while at the same time, they have preserved the rich cultural traditions of Vietnam.

Hung Nguyen (left) *and Hoc Lam* (right) *own this Vietnamese restaurant in Minneapolis, Minnesota. Although Vietnamese immigrants have had to struggle to make their way in the United States, many have become successful businesspeople and contributors to U.S. culture.*

1 VIETNAM

Located in Southeast Asia, Vietnam is bordered on the north by China, on the west by Laos and Cambodia (also known as Kampuchea), and on the south and east by the South China Sea. On a map, Vietnam is long and curving. The main city in the mountainous north—and the nation's capital—is Hanoi. Hue and Da Nang are important secondary cities along the coast of central Vietnam. Ho Chi Minh City, formerly known as Saigon, lies in the fertile Mekong River Delta region of southern Vietnam.

THE LAND

Vietnam receives heavy rainfall during much of the year. This rainfall, plus the hot climate, creates ideal conditions for growing rice. Rice is the country's main crop. Most of the rice farming is done in the Red River Delta in the north and the Mekong River Delta in the south. The river

Many fishers make their living in the Mekong River Delta in Vietnam.

deltas are the areas along the mouths of rivers where the soil is watered by and enriched by the rivers. Most of Vietnam's people live within these regions. Many of them are rice farmers.

In the past, much of Vietnam's interior was tropical rain forest. Many forest areas were wild places where people did not go. Over time, most of the rain forest in Vietnam has been cut down for fuel and timber.

Mountains and plateaus make up most of the rest of the country. Mountain chains run almost the entire length of Vietnam––from the Chinese border in the north to the Mekong River Delta in the south. Hilly terrain and sandy soil make farming in the central region very difficult. Many of the people there rely on hunting, fishing, and gathering wild plants for their food supply.

PEOPLE

By the 200s B.C., the Kinh, or Viet, people from southern China had settled in the northern part of what later became known as Vietnam. Nearby, they encountered groups of people who had been living in the area for centuries. These native peoples included the Hmong, the Yao, the Meo, the Nung, the Thai, and the Jarai. They spoke a number of different languages. Many of them lived in the mountains and highlands.

Most Vietnamese people are ancestors of the Viets. These ethnic Vietnamese make up more than 85 percent of Vietnam's total population of 81 million people. Historically, they have farmed the delta regions and the plains along the coast.

Different minority ethnic groups make up the rest of the Vietnamese population. Many Khmer people live near the border of Cambodia, their ethnic homeland. They mainly farm and fish for a living. People of Chinese descent are found in every Southeast Asian country, including Vietnam. The Chinese originally moved in from China and set up businesses in

A Chinese street vendor sells steamed buns from his cart in Hue, Vietnam.

SOUTHEAST ASIA

Southeast Asia includes the mainland nations of Vietnam, Burma (also known as Myanmar), Cambodia, Thailand, Laos, and peninsular Malaysia. The region also stretches across the South China Sea to the island nations of Indonesia, East Timor, the Philippines, and the Malaysian part of the island of Borneo. The city-state of Singapore and the sultanate of Brunei are also part of Southeast Asia.

Vietnamese cities. At its peak, the Chinese population was about 3 percent of Vietnam's total population.

Vietnamese is the official language of Vietnam. Citizens speak three major dialects, or local forms of the language. These dialects differ little from one another. About twenty languages are spoken among the mountain people. Many of the minority groups speak Vietnamese in addition to their own languages. A number of Vietnamese also speak English, French, Chinese, or Russian.

All of the world's major religions are practiced in Vietnam. These include traditional Asian religions such as Buddhism, Confucianism, Taoism, and Hinduism. Some Vietnamese people practice Christianity, and others follow Islam. Most Vietnamese practice Buddhism or a religious mixture called Tam Giao. Tam Giao means "Triple Religion" and is a mixture of Buddhism, Confucianism, Taoism, and other ancient beliefs. Some Vietnamese practice local religions such as Hoa Hoa and Cao Dai.

ANCIENT KINGDOMS AND DISAGREEMENTS
Throughout its history, Vietnam has struggled against other countries

that have tried to control it. China ruled over much of Vietnam from 111 B.C. to the A.D. 900s. The Chinese tried to convert the Vietnamese people to Chinese ways. The Vietnamese resisted most of these changes. They kept most of their own customs, language, and traditions.

The Vietnamese fought against Chinese control many times. They

TO READ ABOUT MORE HEROES AND HEROINES IN VIETNAMESE HISTORY, VISIT WWW.INAMERICABOOKS.COM FOR LINKS.

THE TRUNG SISTERS

During the early period of Chinese rule, two Vietnamese sisters became famous for carrying out an uprising against Chinese rule. The sisters, Trung Trac and Trung Nhi, had grown up disliking the Chinese invaders. Their father was a Vietnamese military chief.

Trung Trac married Thi Sach, whose father was also a military chief. Thi was also a patriot with strong anti-Chinese feelings. As plans for an uprising were in the works, the Chinese governor of the province, Su Ding, arrested and killed Thi Sach. This enraged Trung Trac. She became even more determined to fight the Chinese.

In A.D. 40, the Trung sisters led the Vietnamese armies, which numbered more than ten thousand troops. The troops were both men and women. The armies stormed through Vietnam, capturing town after town. They succeeded in driving out the Chinese.

The Trung sisters' victory was not long-lived, however. Three years later, the Chinese overtook Vietnam again.

finally forced out the Chinese for good in 939. The Vietnamese kingdom stayed independent from outside rule for six hundred years.

In 1535, however, explorers from the European country of Portugal entered the area. At the time, some European countries looked to Southeast Asia for the chance to expand trading. They were searching for places to sell their goods and to buy Asian goods. The Portuguese were establishing trade routes and trading partners throughout the region. Many Europeans also wanted to bring Christianity to Asia. Portugal introduced the Roman Catholic religion to the Vietnamese. Some Vietnamese began to follow the religion.

At about the same time the Portuguese came, civil war broke out in the region. Rival groups fought for control. In 1545 the Vietnamese kingdom fell and the region came under control of two separate families. General Nguyen Kim and his family took over the southern part of the country. The Trinh family controlled the north. The Nguyen forces built high walls along their northern boundary. The two dynasties, or ruling families, fought throughout the late 1500s and the 1600s. The Trinh dynasty had more troops, elephants, and boats. But the Nguyen had Portuguese weapons and gunpowder. By the late 1600s, a truce between the two groups ended the fighting.

Peace did not bring prosperity. Both dynasties heavily taxed workers and farmers. Life for these poor people became very difficult. The 1700s brought many peasant uprisings, as the poor revolted against their leaders. The year 1771 brought a revolt called the Tay Son Rebellion. It was led by three brothers of the Ho family. First, the brothers ousted the Nguyen dynasty in the south. All of the Nguyen family was killed except for sixteen–year–old Nguyen Anh. Then the rebels overtook the Trinh dynasty in the north.

The brothers who had led the Tay Son Rebellion reunited the country by 1786. They worked to fix the economy. But their reign was short–lived. With help from the French, Nguyen Anh, of the old Nguyen dynasty, gained power over the country in the early 1800s. He adopted the name Gia Long and named the country Nam Viet, or Viet Nam. The new government adopted strict rules. The poor people suffered under forced labor and harsh tax codes. The government also worked closely with French missionaries: Catholic priests who had come to spread their religion in Vietnam.

As the French missionaries converted more people to Catholicism, Vietnamese rulers began to worry. They feared that the growing Catholic community might try to overthrow the government. To prevent this, the government outlawed Christianity in the mid–1800s. In response, French missionaries asked the French military for help. By 1883 French forces had conquered Vietnam. The country became a French colony, run for the profit of the French.

During the period of French control, the Vietnamese suffered many hardships. French

SEIZE THE PROPERTY OF THE RICH AND DISTRIBUTE IT TO THE POOR.

—*slogan of the Tay Son Rebellion*

colonial rulers gave most of the farmland to French colonists and to Vietnamese who were friendly with the colonists. These people gained control of 80 percent of the rice crops in the country. Meanwhile, peasants worked on the estates owned by the wealthy. They earned little money and were forced to pay very high taxes. Few could borrow money to buy land to try to improve their lives. Manufacturing plants were dismantled, leaving workers without jobs.

The longer the French stayed in Vietnam, the more hostility grew. By the early 1900s, some Vietnamese were planning a revolution against the French.

In the early 1900s, small bands of fighters organized themselves across Vietnam in hopes of overthrowing the French.

Some of them formed groups centered on the philosophies of Socialism and Communism. By the 1930s, these groups were recruiting members and planning revolts.

The ideals of Socialism and Communism centered on sharing property and wealth equally among citizens. These ideals were embraced by people who had been beaten down by the French colonial system.

When World War II (1939–1945) broke out, Japanese forces drove European colonists out of Southeast Asia. Japan's ally, Nazi Germany, conquered France in 1940.

While the Japanese occupied Vietnam, a Communist leader named Ho Chi Minh organized an independence movement known as the Viet Minh. The purpose of the group was to fight the Japanese, resist the return of the French, and gain independence for Vietnam.

HO CHI MINH

Ho Chi Minh was born Nguyen Sinh Cung in 1890. Although he was born into a poor peasant family, his father was a scholar. Education was important to his family. Young Nguyen went to school in Hue and in Saigon. In 1911 he began work as part of the crew of a French ship. He traveled to Europe, North America, and Africa. While in France, he studied Communist theory and became a founding member of the French Communist Party. Beginning in the 1930s and 1940s, Ho Chi Minh worked to unite Vietnam as a Communist nation.

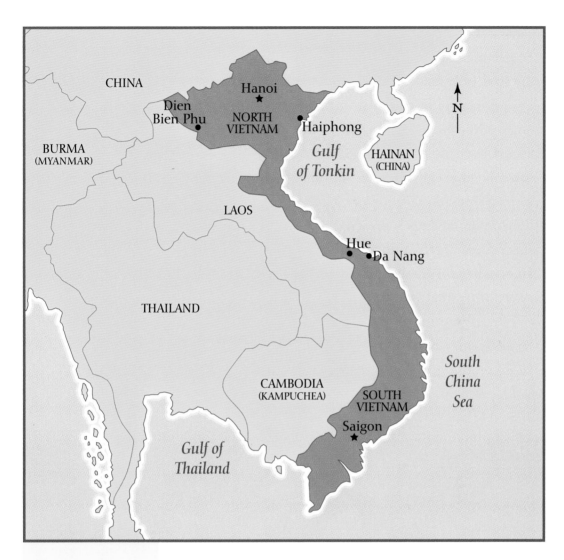

Vietnam was divided in two from 1954 to 1975, when South Vietnam fell to Communist North Vietnam. To download this and other maps, visit www. inamericabooks.com.

NORTH VIETNAM AND SOUTH VIETNAM

By late 1945, both Japan and Germany had been defeated. As World War II was ending, the Viet Minh took control of much of the northern part of Vietnam. That same year, Ho Chi Minh declared independence, setting up the Democratic Republic of Vietnam. The French, however, wanted to take back their colony. French forces managed to regain power in the south.

15

France refused to turn over its control of the south to the new independent state, and fighting broke out.

Vietnamese in both the northern and southern areas of the country opposed French rule. France tried to win over the people by giving southern Vietnam some independence under the rule of Bao Dai, a former emperor. But the Viet Minh refused to accept the continued French presence. Viet Minh forces carried out guerrilla attacks to try to get rid of the French. In guerrilla warfare, fighters often go out alone or in small groups to attack people or places.

French soldiers attack a Viet Minh base of operations in the early 1950s.

YOU CAN KILL TEN OF MY MEN FOR EVERY ONE I KILL OF YOURS, BUT EVEN AT THOSE ODDS, YOU WILL LOSE AND I WILL WIN.

—Ho Chi Minh to the French, late 1940s

They may or may not have a commander. They try to do as much damage to the enemy as they can without being caught.

The war was destructive and costly. Despite its superior weapons and equipment, France could not defeat the Viet Minh. In 1954, after eight years of fighting, the French suffered a major defeat at Dien Bien Phu. The French decided to negotiate. Both sides agreed to meet at a conference in Geneva, Switzerland. They were going to discuss a treaty, or agreement, for peace.

French soldiers protect the landing of French paratroopers at Dien Bien Phu in 1954.

By the 1950s, Communism around the world had become worrisome to many people. Western governments, such as that of the United States, believed that Communist leaders had too much power. They thought that Communist governments did not allow the people enough freedom. They were also concerned that Communist governments were trying to take over other countries. Concerned about the spread of Communism in Asia, the U.S. government had supported the French forces in Vietnam.

The Geneva talks ended with a plan to make Vietnam independent, but not right away. At first, there would be two Vietnams. The country was divided into two zones--north and south. The northern region

In Geneva, Switzerland, a French general signs the treaty as Vietnamese government officials look on.

would have a Communist government under Ho Chi Minh. The southern region would have a non–Communist government headed by Ngo Dinh Diem.

The plan called for reunifying the country and holding national elections by 1956. In the meantime, the northern and southern governments were supposed to end all fighting. But both governments still claimed the right to rule all of Vietnam. They both looked for allies.

North Vietnam received aid from the two most powerful Communist countries—the Soviet Union and China. In the south, the government continued to receive help from the United States. U.S. president Dwight D. Eisenhower promised to make sure that Vietnam would not be a Communist country. He sent U.S. military advisers to train troops in South Vietnam.

Despite the Geneva agreement, conflict between the north and the south continued from 1954 to 1956. The fighting worsened when Ngo Dinh Diem refused to allow a national election in 1956. He claimed that the Communists would not hold a fair election. Diem decided to rid the south of people linked to

Communism. His forces arrested about 100,000 citizens and killed several thousand. The Communists responded by attacking government outposts and seizing areas of South Vietnam. By 1960 all-out war was again under way in Vietnam.

The Vietnam War

The United States became more and more involved in the conflict in Vietnam during the 1960s. President John F. Kennedy sent millions of dollars' worth of weapons and military equipment to South Vietnam. But Diem was an unpopular leader. His government was cruel and harsh, and many people did not support it. Thousands joined Communist liberation groups and guerrilla armies to fight against Diem's government. An army called the Viet Cong joined the Viet Minh in their fight against the South Vietnamese government.

Buddhist leaders led protests that brought many people to the streets. Special forces under Diem rounded up and jailed thousands of protesters. In November 1963,

Ngo was assassinated, and General Duong Van Minh took over.

In 1964 U.S. president Lyndon B. Johnson began sending U.S. troops to fight the Communists in Vietnam. By 1965 more than 200,000 U.S. troops were in Vietnam. Three years later, the number had risen to more than 500,000. Despite the U.S. forces and their high-quality equipment, South Vietnam couldn't defeat the Viet Minh and the Viet Cong.

The war continued, and it was bitter and bloody. Many thousands of people were dying on both sides. Whole villages were destroyed. City buildings crumbled, and no one

We seem bent upon saving the Vietnamese from Ho Chi Minh, even if we have to kill them and demolish their country to do it.

—Senator George McGovern, speech to U.S. Senate, April 25, 1967

A South Vietnamese soldier threatens a Viet Cong prisoner with a knife in an effort to force him to reveal the location of his unit.

could work or farm. Food was scarce. Many families lost loved ones. Many people in the United States were deeply opposed to the war. By the early 1970s, the United States was looking for a way to end the war.

In January 1973, an agreement involving the Viet Minh, the Viet Cong, South Vietnam, and the United States was finally signed in Paris. The agreement was meant to end fighting in Vietnam. The United States removed its troops from Vietnam in March. Soon after, however, war broke out again between North Vietnam and South Vietnam. Finally, in April 1975, troops from North Vietnam overran the city of Saigon in South Vietnam. The war was over, and the

IF ONLY THE CHILDREN COULD HAVE HAD THE MOON AND THE STARS, THE FLOWERS AND THE BUTTERFLIES, INSTEAD OF THE WAR.

—Phong Trieu, "The School on the Front Line," Between Two Fires, 1970

entire country came under Communist rule.

The cost of the drawn-out war was high for all involved. More than one million North and South Vietnamese troops were killed, and the number of civilian deaths is unknown. Vietnamese people

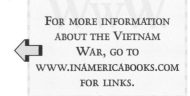
FOR MORE INFORMATION ABOUT THE VIETNAM WAR, GO TO WWW.INAMERICABOOKS.COM FOR LINKS.

throughout the country were left wondering and worrying about what would happen next.

AMERICAN REACTIONS

During the 1970s, the war in Vietnam became a subject of bitter debate in the United States. Members of Congress argued about whether it was right to be fighting a war without actually having officially declared war. Many people believed that the United States had no good reason to be fighting in Vietnam. Students protested *(right)*, sometimes violently, against a conflict that they saw as immoral. They believed the United

States had no business trying to control another country's fate. Some young men drafted to serve in the U.S. Army chose instead to flee to Canada. Others believed that America had a responsibility to combat the spread of Communism in Southeast Asia.

2 VIETNAMESE REFUGEES

As the war ended, many Vietnamese people decided to flee from their country. The first Vietnamese refugees left during April 1975, as South Vietnam fell to the north. These people were mainly government and military officials who had worked with U.S. forces. These officials fled with their families. Vietnamese wives of U.S. troops who had been stationed in South Vietnam and their Vietnamese American children also escaped. So did employees of U.S. companies in Vietnam. These people all wanted to leave because they were concerned about their safety under the North Vietnamese government. Having fought against the Communists, many South Vietnamese believed that the new government would arrest or even kill them.

THE FIRST REFUGEES

The U.S. government had formed a plan to evacuate people from South Vietnam. More than 40,000 persons were evacuated from Vietnam in April alone. In the first few months following the fall of South Vietnam, about 150,000 people went to the United States. About 50,000 more fled to other countries.

Early in the month of April, U.S. president Gerald Ford okayed a project called Operation Babylift. The plan called for the evacuation of children and babies that government agencies were caring for in orphanages. Using airplanes and helicopters, more than three thousand children of varying ages were airlifted out of Saigon. About two thousand of these children were adopted by families in the United States. Families in Canada, Australia, and Europe adopted the others.

The Vietnamese refugees who entered the United States in the first wave were mainly highly educated and relatively wealthy. Almost three-fourths of them had attended high school, and one-fifth had studied at a university. These people were generally

OPERATION BABYLIFT BEGINS WITH TRAGEDY

The first flight out of Saigon in the Operation Babylift mission met with disaster. An explosion rocked the plane in midair soon after take-off. The pilots crash-landed near Saigon. About half of the passengers—including three hundred children—died in the crash. People running the Operation Babylift program were horrified. But they knew they must go on. Planes and helicopters continued to evacuate the children, including those who survived the crash.

young—under forty years of age. But few of them had ever lived outside of Vietnam.

Some of the first Vietnamese refugees made it quickly to the United States. Most of these people spoke French or English or both. Many had contacts in the U.S. government who could help them. These people were often able to avoid long stays in refugee camps. Some went straight to the United States. But most refugees had to spend some time in camps called reception centers.

RECEPTION CENTERS

The majority of the first-wave refugees had to pass through reception centers on their way to the United States. Many were first taken to U.S. military bases in Thailand or in the Philippines. They then went on to Wake Island or to Guam, two U.S. islands in the Pacific. Their final destination was the U.S. mainland. The original reception centers in America were located at Camp Pendleton, California; Fort Chafee, Arkansas;

We came to U.S. territory at night. Despite our excited state, darkness prohibited a clear view of part of a country in which we were going to spend the rest of our lives. At that late hour the island of Guam seemed to consist of thousands of lights.

Our ship dropped anchor about 3 A.M., July 5, 1975. We, nine thousand people, gathered on deck, confused at first. Then, one by one, we climbed down the rope ladder. One man led his son by the hand, another carried his old father; one carried a briefcase, another wrapped his property in a blanket and another loosely held a water container in his hand. . . . These poor people were warmly received.

—Vo Phien,
"The Key"

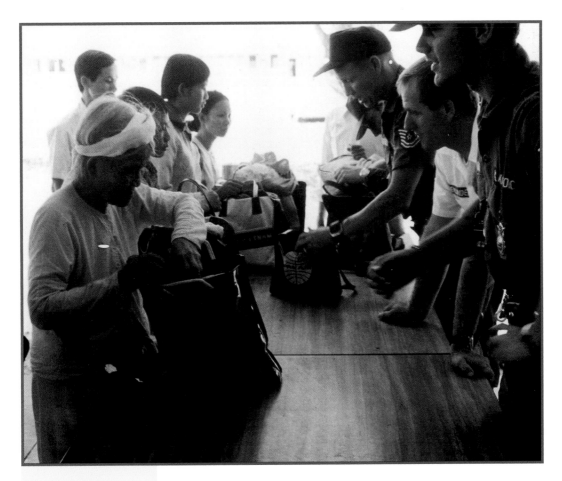

U.S. customs officers check the baggage of Vietnamese refugees at a reception center.

WANT TO READ VIETNAMESE LITERATURE AND POETRY? VISIT WWW.INAMERICABOOKS.COM FOR LINKS.

Elgin Air Force Base, Florida; and Fort Indiantown Gap, Pennsylvania.

In the camps, the refugees were interviewed and given medical examinations. Camp officials held classes to teach English. They provided information on U.S. culture. They tried to offer practical instruction, such as how to find a job in the United States. To leave the camps and settle permanently in the United States, Vietnamese persons or families had to have a sponsor. A sponsor could be a person, a family, or an organization approved by the U.S. government.

LIFE IN A REFUGEE CAMP: TRUE STORIES

Mai was fourteen when she, her parents, and her five brothers and sisters arrived at a refugee camp. Having survived a perilous trip by boat, Mai's family felt lucky to be alive and at the camp. They didn't realize that camp life would be so hard.

In order to go on to America, each refugee family had to have a sponsor in the United States. Although Mai and her family had friends who had been in the U.S Army, they didn't know how to contact them. Mai remembers being questioned by immigration officials in the camp about her reasons for leaving Vietnam. The officials interrogated her father about his background to make sure he was not allied with the Communist government. They also were trying to match the family with a sponsoring agency in the United States. Because of the huge number of refugees needing help, the search for a sponsor took much longer than Mai had expected.

The eleven months that Mai's family spent in the camp were both boring and frightening. Because there was nothing for most of the people to do, some became restless and frustrated. Gangs formed, and attacks by Vietnamese on other Vietnamese took place frequently. Mai was afraid to leave her family's hut after dark for fear of the gangs. The uncertainty of where and when her family would be going added to her nervousness.

Finally, Mai's father found out that a sponsor had been found. Even then, it seemed another long wait until Mai and her family actually boarded a plane for St. Louis, Missouri. She remembers her first day in the United States as one of the happiest in her life.

As a teenager, Phong left Vietnam for a world that was unknown to him. During his schooling, he had learned about the history of Vietnam and the surrounding countries but little about the West.

When Phong first entered a refugee camp, he was surprised to find a school for young people his age. In classes, workers from international agencies taught cultural orientation—the way of life in the countries that were the refugees' final destinations. Phong attended lectures on housing, communication, personal hygiene, and food. He also took a class to learn English.

Even with school, life in the camp was boring. Phong didn't have enough to do to keep him busy. He spent a lot of time gambling with small odds and ends that he collected around the camp. The months dragged on, and almost two years passed before Phong was able to leave for America.

In the United States, Phong moved around a great deal at first. He finally located an uncle who had established a small business in which Phong could work. Phong worked full-time and put himself through college to become an electrical engineer.

Life in refugee camps was boring, frustrating, and sometimes even dangerous for children like these two boys in a refugee camp in Thailand. For more stories of Vietnamese immigrants and refugees, visit www.inamericabooks.com for links.

SPONSORS

The U.S. government asked individuals and private agencies to volunteer as sponsors for the new refugees. Many families and organizations offered to help, sponsoring tens of thousands of refugees. Sponsors located housing and helped the refugees learn basic English. They helped refugees find jobs and got the children started in schools.

In 1975 the U.S. policy was to settle the newcomers in different locations around the country. That way, a sudden rush of refugees would not overwhelm one local or state government. U.S. officials also believed that, this way, the Vietnamese would adjust more quickly to American society. If scattered, rather than concentrated in Vietnamese communities, officials thought the refugees would

These refugees escaped Vietnam in an airplane. Here they arrive in an Oakland, California, airport.

be forced to become "American" more quickly.

Many Americans worked hard to welcome the Vietnamese refugees into the United States. One reason was a sense of responsibility toward the refugees. The U.S. government had fought for them and failed. The United States, at least partially, was to blame for their having to leave their homeland.

SECOND-WAVE REFUGEES

During the war, much of the fighting took place in rural areas. As a result, many people living in the Vietnamese countryside had been forced to leave their homes and farms. Many had looked for

The Catholic Church sponsored some Vietnamese immigrants. This family was brought to Pittsburgh, Pennsylvania, by its Catholic sponsors.

safety in cities, especially Saigon. As a result, Saigon (since renamed Ho Chi Minh City) was severely overpopulated. The Vietnamese government decided to return people to the countryside. New villages were planned in regions where few people lived. These areas were called New Economic Zones.

During the late 1970s, hundreds of thousands of Vietnamese were forced to leave Ho Chi Minh City for the countryside. Under the strict supervision of Communist officials, these people built villages, worked in the fields, and tried to adapt to a new rural life. But many of the people who were forced to resettle were not used to such a life. People who had worked as secretaries, bankers, and storekeepers were not physically or mentally prepared for farming.

Some died from the hardships involved in creating the new farming areas. Many refused to accept the difficult new lifestyle and tried to return to Ho Chi Minh City. The more the people resisted, the harsher the government became in enforcing its resettlement plan. A growing number of Vietnamese people felt they had to leave the country. They made up the second great wave of Vietnamese refugees to head for the United States.

People fled Ho Chi Minh City in overloaded trucks, carts, and bicycles.

Many Vietnamese people fled their native land by boat during the late 1970s. This tiny vessel carried 326 refugees.

BOAT PEOPLE

Unable to take flights out of Vietnam after 1975, most of the refugees fleeing in the second wave had to use boats. The term "boat people" is used for those who escaped from Vietnam by boat. Every kind of floatable vessel was used to ferry refugees. People rode in small fishing boats, large cargo ships, homemade rafts, and empty oil drums.

Boats were commonly jammed with three to four times the number of people they could safely carry. Many of the vessels were old and unsafe. The boat people escaped Vietnam hoping to land at the nearest possible port outside the country. They risked their lives just leaving Vietnam, because it was illegal for them to leave.

THE BOAT PEOPLE: TRUE STORIES

Van was born in Saigon and spent his childhood there. When his family decided to leave Vietnam, they traveled about one hundred miles to the coast to board a boat headed for Malaysia. Van remembers fifty people crowding into the small boat, with everyone afraid and anxious to leave the country.

After six days of sailing on the South China Sea, it became apparent that the small boat was lost. On three occasions, the people on Van's boat sighted large merchant vessels passing by and tried to get them to stop. Only once did those on a larger ship even wave to them, but no one stopped to aid the refugees.

The boat people soon ran out of water and then ran out of food.

The ordeal was especially hard on the small children on board. People began to die. Their bodies were wrapped in old clothes and put into the water.

After fifteen days at sea, the small boat was spotted by an Indonesian freighter, and those still alive were rescued. Of the fifty people who had begun the trip, twelve had died during the voyage.

Conditions on the boats that took refugees from Vietnam were crowded and uncomfortable.

Thien was sixteen years old when he became a refugee. He and his family left Vietnam aboard small boats. His father, grandfather, and other family members crammed onto one crowded vessel, and Thien boarded another. About three days out to sea, the two boats lost sight of each other. Thien was worried but believed he could find his family once his boat arrived safely on land.

During a huge storm one night, the fragile, overcrowded boat that Thien was on began to break up. Thien tried to help the older people hold onto pieces of the ship that would keep them afloat.

Suddenly, Thien was washed overboard. He struggled in the high waves to get back to what was left of the boat, but he couldn't get close to it. As he drifted away, he watched many of his fellow passengers drown. By the time the storm ended, Thien had been carried miles from where the boat had sunk. He treaded water for what seemed like days and was finally picked up by an American ship.

Living in the United States, Thien has never been able to locate his family and does not know if they are alive or dead.

Huu was only six years old when he and his family left Vietnam. On the way to Thailand, his family's boat was attacked by pirates. The boat's captain was shot, and the pirates took all the food and water and several of the young girls from the refugee boat, including Huu's sister.

Two days later, a second pirate ship stopped the boat and took the people's clothes. Suffering from hunger, thirst, cold, and fear, the refugees tried to find land. Because of rough seas, the boat people finally had to abandon the ship and swim ashore. Huu's father jumped into the water with his son, and they were washed onto the beach. Huu and his parents have never heard from his sister.

The boat people endured many horrors in their efforts to leave Vietnam by sea. They were able to take few, if any, of their possessions with them. And most were forced to pay very high prices even for standing room on a vessel.

Conditions aboard the boats were often miserable. Many of the passengers had little or no food and water. People were threatened by terrible storms on the South China Sea. They also faced danger from pirates and Vietnamese coast patrols. Pirates would attack and board refugee ships and take what few possessions the people had left. They often took what little food and water was on board. Sometimes they beat or killed the men. They often assaulted the women. Pirates commonly then left the helpless refugees adrift, sometimes on a sinking ship.

Many boat people died at sea. Estimates of their losses range from 40,000 to 200,000 people. Yet despite the dangers, U.S. officials reported as many as 14,000 refugees escaping Vietnam per month during this period.

In 1978 and 1979, many of the boat people who left Vietnam were people of Chinese descent. While ethnic Vietnamese had left the country illegally, ethnic Chinese were forced to leave. Vietnam and China were enemies at this time, and the Vietnamese government wanted all the ethnic Chinese out. More than 200,000 Vietnamese people of Chinese descent crossed the border into China. Another 300,000 became boat people.

COUNTRIES OF FIRST ASYLUM

For those who survived the boat journeys, the major difficulty became finding somewhere to land. The places where the refugees first landed after leaving Vietnam were called countries of first asylum. Because of their geographic closeness to Vietnam, common countries of first asylum for the refugees were Thailand, Malaysia, and the Philippines.

Many countries in Southeast Asia, however, did not welcome the Vietnamese refugees. These countries were already overwhelmed by their own problems. They did not want the burden of caring for thousands of refugees. Also, the risk that refugees might carry disease and health-related problems made them unwelcome guests.

The first boat people sailed south from Vietnam toward Malaysia. But the Malaysian navy set up sea blockades (barriers made with ships) to prevent the refugees from landing. This forced them to sail elsewhere. The government of Thailand tried to discourage the boat people from landing in Thailand by failing to arrest Thai pirates who were attacking the refugee boats. These actions forced the refugees to make their escapes in another direction. Even cargo

A boatload of Vietnamese refugees sails toward Malaysia in 1978.

ship captains were afraid to pick up the boatloads of starving refugees they found. They feared they would be unable to unload them at any nearby port.

Nevertheless, many boat people were able to reach other nations. But this was only one leg on a long and difficult journey. Very few boat people would be allowed to settle in these countries permanently. They had to live in camps until they could be taken to other countries for permanent settlement.

The one port in the Southeast Asian region that welcomed the refugees was the British–held port of Hong Kong. Hong Kong set up camps for the refugees with the aid of the International Red Cross and the United Nations High Commission for Refugees (UNHCR). Hong Kong became the second port of

THE SEAS WERE INFESTED WITH PIRATES, AND BEYOND THE PIRATES LAY A STRING OF SQUALID REFUGEE CAMPS ALREADY FILLED TO OVERFLOWING.

—*Troung Nhu Tang,*
A Viet Cong
Memoir

Refugees who ended up in the Hong Kong camps were considered lucky to have a place to live, even though the camps were crowded.

asylum for thousands of refugees who had first landed in Malaysia or other countries.

Life in refugee camps was not easy. The vast number of people requiring help made it difficult to meet everyone's needs. Food and water were not always plentiful, schooling was not adequate, and few jobs were available. There was very little to do in the camps. People sat idle, waiting. Camp residents applied for entry into the United States or other countries. But they often waited months, sometimes even years, to have their applications approved.

Final destinations for Vietnamese refugees included countries all over the world. Australia, Canada, China, and France accepted large numbers of boat people. The United States took in more than all other countries combined.

ORDERLY DEPARTURE PROGRAM

In 1979 the UNHCR commission reached an agreement with the Vietnamese government that allowed Vietnamese citizens to immigrate to the United States. To do this, the UNHCR set up the Orderly Departure Program (ODP).

Vietnamese people who wished to settle in the United States could apply for permission to leave Vietnam under the ODP. They were granted permission to move to America under one of three categories established by the ODP and approved by the U.S. Department of State.

Vietnamese refugees wait in a Ho Chi Minh airport. This group of people gained permission to enter the United States through the ODP.

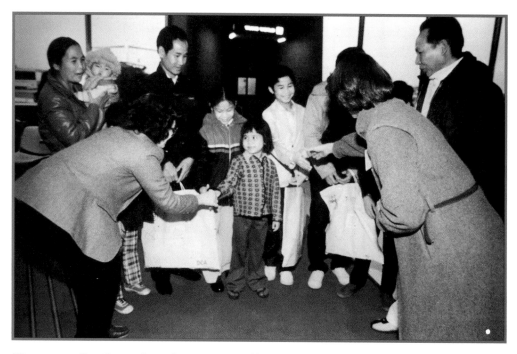

Vietnamese families such as this one were able to make a new start in the United States thanks to the ODP.

Category 1 included Vietnamese who were close family members of persons already living in the United States. "Close family members" were spouses, sons, daughters, parents, grandparents, and unmarried grandchildren. People living in the United States could apply to the program on behalf of their family members still in Vietnam. Category 2 included ethnic Vietnamese who had worked for the U.S. government in Vietnam for at least one year.

Category 3 included persons who were able to show a close tie to the United States. This broad category was designed to provide entry to America for former employees of U.S. companies, former students who had studied in the United States, people with one American parent or grandparent, and people who had suffered or had been punished because of their former association with the U.S. government or its armed forces.

In September 1986, the 50,000th refugee in the Orderly Departure Program entered the United States. In 1988 the U.S. government arranged with the Vietnamese government for 100,000 political prisoners—people arrested for disagreeing with a government—to be released through the ODP. Through the ODP, immigrants continued to come to the United States from Vietnam throughout the 1990s.

In the past years, relations between the United States and Vietnam have improved dramatically. But there are still ongoing debates about people who want to leave Vietnam. The Vietnamese government says that many of these people are leaving illegally and have no reason to fear being harmed. The people trying to leave say they lack food, access to clean water, schools, and roads. Many of them live in the central highlands and belong to one of Vietnam's minority ethnic groups. The UNHCR negotiates with the Vietnamese government over many of these cases.

FIND LINKS TO LEARN MORE ABOUT MODERN VIETNAM AT WWW.INAMERICABOOKS.COM.

Poverty has plagued Vietnam for decades. Large cities such as Ho Chi Minh City and Hue have large numbers of homeless people (below).

3 VIETNAMESE IN AMERICA

Vietnamese Americans have made amazing strides in getting ahead in American society. But they didn't do so without struggles along the way. Most arrived with nothing more than the clothes on their backs. Yet many have worked hard to become successful members of their communities.

ADAPTATION

Many refugees had trouble getting over the emotions of leaving their homeland after a violent, frightening war. Most struggled to adapt to the American culture and a new language and lifestyle.

Children adopted into American families had to learn a new life without the old culture to fall back upon. They had to adapt to a new country and a new family as well as cope with the loss of their Vietnamese families. Most also faced the challenges of looking different and speaking a different language.

Most Vietnamese refugees came with few, if any, possessions and little or no money. Many received financial help from the U.S. government. Some Vietnamese received contributions of money, clothing, and other goods and services from their sponsors. Most refugees, however, managed to get along well after their first few years in America. Ambitious and hardworking, many found good jobs in little time.

Many Vietnamese people who moved to the United States during the 1970s have become successful businesspeople. These four men own a Vietnamese restaurant in Los Angeles, California.

Vietnamese Americans formed various Vietnamese American organizations in the 1970s and 1980s. Most are still thriving. Broadly, their purpose is to help Vietnamese American people succeed in America and to preserve the Vietnamese culture. Some of the associations promote the businesses or professions of their members. Others work to ease the feeling of isolation in a new land.

At first, these associations provided numerous services. They offered classes in English, job counseling, housing assistance, and even driving lessons. They also acted as sponsors for refugees. Some served as centers of information for locating Vietnamese persons in the United States. They also worked to reunite families that had been separated. In addition, the associations introduced the Vietnamese culture to the host American communities. For example, they coordinated the celebration of Tet—the Vietnamese New Year— and invited the general public to attend.

The Vietnamese American Society works to promote Vietnamese culture, enhance business relations between the United States and Vietnam, and

Vietnamese teenagers work together to perform the Dragon Dance, an important part of any Tet celebration.

serve the Vietnamese community in the United States. The Vietnamese American Council was founded to help Vietnamese Americans start businesses or get jobs. It also works to preserve Vietnamese culture. The Vietnamese–American Public Affairs Committee helps Vietnamese Americans get involved in U.S. politics. The National Alliance of Vietnamese American Service Agencies also works to help Vietnamese Americans succeed economically and politically.

NEW HOMES IN THE UNITED STATES

At first the U.S. Immigration Service settled Vietnamese refugees across the country. That policy was later changed. The refugees' adjustment was made harder by the absence of a Vietnamese community, by a feeling of isolation, and by the difficulties of living far from family members.

In scattering the refugees around the country, the government had broken up large families. Once the refugees were settled and had become self-sufficient, they often

Though I belong in the post-war generation by age, my life has been and continues to be profoundly affected by the Vietnam War. It is like a heavy baggage that is assigned to me along with the refugee status as I came to America fifteen years ago.

—Hoaithi P. Nguyen, Los Angeles, California, Postwar Generation, December 31, 1996

relocated to be reunited with other family members. Some moved to cities with established Vietnamese communities, such as Los Angeles, Seattle, and Dallas. The big cities also offered more job opportunities to the refugees. Other refugees relocated to New Orleans. That city was attractive because of its hot climate, similar to that of Vietnam. And because New Orleans has a strong French culture, it attracted refugees looking for something familiar.

By 1986 all fifty states had refugees from Vietnam. The largest populations settled in California, Texas, and Washington. The concentration of Vietnamese in major urban areas continued in the 1990s and into the new millennium.

Little Saigon, in the Westminster area of Orange

CHECK OUT
WWW.INAMERICABOOKS.COM
FOR LINKS TO A GLIMPSE
OF LIFE IN CALIFORNIA'S
LITTLE SAIGON.

County, California, has a large Vietnamese American population, with more than 350,000 people. More than 125,000 Vietnamese

Though the largest number of Vietnamese immigrants settled in California, Vietnamese American communities are thriving in all fifty states. Visit www.inamericabooks.com to download this map.

Americans live in San Jose, California. In Houston, Texas, more than 100,000 Vietnamese Americans have settled. Los Angeles, California, is also home to many Vietnamese Americans. Overall, more than 1.5 million Vietnamese Americans live in the United States.

WORKING

Soon after most Vietnamese refugees arrived in the United States, they began seeking jobs. Their need for employment was great, because they didn't have homes, cars, or even possessions that most people take for granted. Many had to accept low-paying jobs. They worked with the hope of saving money for education or to support other family members. Many refugees brought with them a strong work ethic. These qualities sometimes caused conflicts and misunderstandings between Americans and the newcomers.

In Houston, Texas, for example, a number of convenience store jobs were available from midnight to seven o'clock in the morning. Although the pay was low and the hours were inconvenient, many Vietnamese people took these jobs. Some Houston residents thought the refugees were taking jobs away from people who had lived in America for a long time. The Vietnamese, however, felt they had accepted jobs that no one else wanted.

Another example of a misunderstanding involving jobs occurred in Biloxi, Mississippi, a city located on

the Gulf of Mexico. Vietnamese refugees had bought boats and began fishing there for shrimp. They worked long, hard hours. To get an early start each morning, they even lived or slept on their boats.

The custom in the coast region is for fishers to have certain areas of the water for their own use. The Vietnamese did not understand that. They fished anywhere there were shrimp to be caught. This offended the local shrimpers. Some residents became so angry that they wanted to force the Vietnamese to leave. Finally, the local fishing community figured out a way to communicate with the Vietnamese and solve the problem.

Many refugees had to accept jobs far below those they had held in Vietnam. Some professionals couldn't

Americans have sometimes misinterpreted the intentions of Vietnamese workers and business owners, such as this shopkeeper in Garden Grove, California. Some Americans feel threatened by the Vietnamese ability to work long or odd hours.

put their skills to use in America because they couldn't speak English. Others found that the job qualifications in the United States were different from those in Vietnam. Studying English or learning different business practices helped many of those refugees to get back on their feet in the workplace. Many Vietnamese Americans have excelled in their professions.

FAMILY AND RELIGION

Many Vietnamese refugee families struggled to adjust to the American way of life. In the United States, people traditionally view "family" as a small group—father and/or mother and children. In Vietnam, "family" means parents and children, grandparents, married children, aunts, uncles, and a variety of other relatives. In some

Although some Vietnamese refugees haven't been able to work in their chosen fields, others have found immense professional success. Some, such as this congressional candidate, have pursued political careers.

cases, the entire family lives in the same house.

The family is the center of Vietnamese society, and it is the responsibility of every member to help the family survive. But the size of an extended Vietnamese family can make it difficult to find housing in America. Families want to establish themselves as close units but often cannot find housing large enough to hold twenty or thirty relatives.

In Vietnamese culture, older people are highly respected. Young people are always expected to seek the advice of older relatives. Children are taught to listen to and accept the decisions of their elders. In the traditional American family, however, individual members are more independent. In the United States, many children are taught and advised by their parents in a less structured way.

Many young Vietnamese Americans have had problems with the cultural differences. As they have become friends with young Americans, they have seen the more informal relationships they have with their families. The Vietnamese American youths have pushed for more independence—something their Vietnamese parents found difficult to accept. Elders have sometimes become

Many Vietnamese Americans would prefer to live with extended family but are forced to live in smaller family groups.

Young Vietnamese Americans have been eager to embrace American culture, fashion, and customs. This has put distance between Vietnamese American youth and their more traditional older relatives.

angry and have tried to enforce their control. Vietnamese American teens have sometimes rebelled. A few young Vietnamese Americans have turned to drugs and gangs.

As the years have passed, most Vietnamese Americans have settled into life in the United States. Many families have made compromises, keeping some old traditions while adapting in other ways to American customs. Second and third generations of Vietnamese Americans have succeeded in ways that first–generation refugees hadn't thought possible. The Vietnamese Americans have become a strong and thriving community in the United States.

Religion plays an important role in Vietnamese culture. The majority of Vietnamese people are Buddhists. Buddhism originated in India and spread to Southeast Asia between 100 B.C. and A.D. 500. This religion focuses on giving up attachment to worldly things to achieve peace and happiness. Vietnamese and other Asians following Buddhism have started religious centers in the United States. Communities of Buddhist monks and nuns have been set up throughout the nation.

FIND LINKS TO LEARN MORE ABOUT VIETNAMESE PEOPLE, CULTURE, AND HISTORY AT WWW.INAMERICABOOKS.COM.

The Chinese philosophy of Confucianism has had a strong impact on the people and the history of Vietnam. Confucianism considers the family the foundation of the social order. Its ideals include kindness and tolerance. Another religion, Taoism, was founded by a Chinese philosopher. Its teachings have been a part of Vietnamese culture for more than two thousand years. Taoism teaches that humankind needs

Confucian priests perform a ritual ceremony in Los Angeles as part of a Tet celebration.

to find harmony by returning to natural ways of life. It stresses harmony between individuals and nature. Those who practice Taoism avoid all forms of confrontation.

The blending of a variety of religious beliefs is common among the Vietnamese. For example, a person might be a Buddhist who also follows the teachings of Confucianism and seeks harmony through Taoism.

A minority of the Vietnamese refugees in the United States came as Christians. Most of them are members of the Roman Catholic Church. The Vietnamese who came to the United States as Catholics have adapted well to American Catholicism. A number of Vietnamese priests came with the refugees. In several American cities, Vietnamese worshipers can attend services conducted in their native language.

EDUCATION AND LANGUAGE

The Vietnamese culture places a high value on education. As

Vietnamese American Catholics dress in traditional clothing at a special Mass held during Tet.

persons of knowledge, teachers are considered some of the most important members of society.

Before Europeans arrived in Vietnam, people there embraced the Confucian system of education. This system focused on memorization. Students memorized large amounts of material and then took exams, in which they quoted the memorized material. If they passed, they could improve their employment and social standing. Anyone—farmer or aristocrat—could take the exams.

Vietnamese schoolchildren in Little Saigon, California, recite the Pledge of Allegiance. Adjusting to schooling methods in the United States is challenging for some refugees.

In Vietnam, education was an important part of a child's life. Teachers in these schools were considered role models as well as instructors. Discipline was a key part of education. Children were expected to show respect. They were taught not to question what the instructors said or did.

When Vietnamese refugees began attending American schools in the 1970s and 1980s, most children experienced a different type of education than they had known in Vietnam. In Vietnam, children listen to and learn from the teacher, who is always correct. In America, students learn from the teacher but are also taught to think for themselves. Despite these differences, many young Vietnamese have adapted well and are excelling in school.

The most important and hardest task for a new refugee is learning English. For some people, such as immigrants from Europe or from Mexico, it is not quite as difficult to learn English as it is for people whose first language is Vietnamese. Vietnamese uses characters, not an alphabet, for writing. So many Vietnamese had to learn the English alphabet. The Vietnamese language contains six basic tones, and the tone of each word is part of the meaning of the word. In English, which is not tonal, one word can be used to mean many things. For the non–English speaker, this can be very confusing and a source of difficulty in attempting to learn English.

Even the way names are written is different in the two languages. In Vietnamese the family name is written first to emphasize the importance of the family. In the United States, the family name is written last. An American man would write his name John Michael Doe. But in Vietnam, he would be Doe John Michael.

When a Vietnamese woman marries, she keeps her maiden name and also uses her husband's name. For example, if Le Thi Ba married Nguyen Pham Binh, she would still be called Le Thi Ba in informal situations. But on formal occasions, such as during a ceremony, she would be called Mrs. Nguyen Pham Binh.

To avoid confusion, some Vietnamese in the United States have adopted the American system and put their family names last instead of first. There are only about thirty family names for all Vietnamese. The

MANY PEOPLE ARE INTERESTED IN LEARNING ABOUT THEIR FAMILY'S HISTORY. THIS STUDY IS CALLED GENEALOGY. IF YOU'D LIKE TO LEARN ABOUT YOUR OWN GENEALOGY AND HOW YOUR ANCESTORS CAME TO AMERICA, VISIT WWW.INAMERICABOOKS.COM FOR TIPS AND LINKS TO HELP YOU GET STARTED. THERE YOU'LL ALSO FIND TIPS ON RESEARCHING NAMES IN YOUR FAMILY HISTORY.

most common one is Nguyen (pronounced "wihn"), which is used by almost half the population.

CUSTOMS

The basic customs of Vietnamese life have been handed down from generation to generation. In the United States, refugees also have handed down traditions and beliefs to their children and grandchildren.

Every year, Vietnamese Americans across the United States gather in various locations to celebrate the Tet festival. In Vietnam, Tet is like the American Thanksgiving, Christmas, and New Year's Day combined. The celebration traditionally begins on the first day of the first month of the lunar year (usually in January or February) and lasts several days. Huge Tet festivals in the United States are held in San Jose and Westminster, California; Washington, D.C.; Houston, Texas; Seattle, Washington; and many other locations. The festivals feature food, costumes, games, music, dancing, sports tournaments, parades, fireworks, shows, rides, and more.

Vietnamese foods have become quite popular in the United States. In a Vietnamese restaurant, you will be able to sample from multiple dishes of fish, seafood, pork, and vegetables alongside nuoc mam (fish sauce), peanut sauce, and spiced cucumber and pickle slices. Popular foods include *pho* (beef soup), *nem ran* (spring rolls), and *cha ca* (fish balls). Many dishes include mung beans, bean sprouts, bamboo shoots, gingerroot, lemongrass, rice and noodles, and spices and fresh herbs. Tea is served throughout the day in Vietnamese households.

Vietnamese cuisine includes many dishes that combine fresh and cooked ingredients, creating varied textures and tastes.

RICE NOODLE SALAD

This is a favorite dish throughout Vietnam, where it is eaten primarily in the summer. To learn how to prepare other Vietnamese dishes, visit www.inamericabooks.com for links.

3 C. WATER

1 7-OZ. PACKAGE RICE NOODLES

2 C. LETTUCE, SHREDDED

$^1/_2$ CUCUMBER, PEELED AND SLICED

2 CARROTS, PEELED AND SHREDDED

2 TBSP. VEGETABLE OIL

$^1/_2$ ONION, PEELED AND SLICED

1 LB. PORK LOIN, THINLY SLICED

1 TBSP. DRIED LEMONGRASS, SOAKED
  IN HOT WATER FOR 30 MINUTES

1 CLOVE GARLIC, MINCED AND
  FINELY CHOPPED

$^1/_2$ TSP. SUGAR

$^1/_4$ TSP. PEPPER

2 TBSP. FISH SAUCE

$^1/_2$ C. CHOPPED ROASTED PEANUTS

1. In a large saucepan, bring water to a boil. Add rice noodles and boil for 4 to 5 minutes. Drain noodles in a colander. Allow to cool.

2. When noodles are cool, use a sharp knife or scissors to cut them into shorter lengths.

3. Divide rice noodles among 4 small bowls. Divide lettuce, cucumber, and carrots and add to each bowl. Set aside.

4. In a large skillet, heat oil over high heat for 1 minute. Add onion and cook, stirring frequently, for 2 to 3 minutes, or until tender.

5. Add meat and stir. Add lemongrass, garlic, sugar, and pepper. Cook, stirring frequently, 3 to 5 minutes, or until meat is thoroughly cooked. Add fish sauce and stir well.

6. Divide cooked meat mixture among the 4 bowls and sprinkle 2 tbsp. peanuts over each.

Serves 4

PEACE

Relations between the United States and Vietnam have improved in the recent past. In 1989 American television producers went to produce a film in Vietnam. There they met Nguyen Ngoc Hung, a veteran of the war who had fought for North Vietnam. Nguyen's kind, compassionate character made an impact on the Americans, who invited him to the United States. While in America, Nguyen visited Neillsville, Wisconsin, to see the Highground Veterans Memorial—a tribute to Americans who fought in the Vietnam War. Nguyen was deeply affected by the memorial. He returned to the United States in 1993 and met Mike Boehm, a war veteran active in veterans' affairs. Boehm and Nguyen discussed plans for a peace park in Vietnam. The My

NEARLY THIRTY YEARS AGO, AMERICANS DID SOMETHING TERRIBLE IN . . . MY LAI. HERE IS A CHANCE TO DO SOMETHING BEAUTIFUL IN THAT SAME PLACE.

—W. D. Ehrhart, Vietnam veteran and poet

The Highground Veterans Memorial (below) *became the inspiration for My Lai Peace Park in Vietnam.*

MY LAI PEACE PARK

My Lai Peace Park is named after a tragedy of the Vietnam War. In 1968 U.S. troops entered the village of My Lai in search of enemy soldiers. There weren't any, but the soldiers went on a rampage, killing old men, women, and children and burning homes. In four hours, 504 innocent people were slaughtered. One of the military leaders involved in the atrocity was brought to trial and jailed, but he was released a few years later. Naming the peace park after this village symbolizes forgiveness and hope for peace in the future.

Lai Peace Park Project was born. In 1995 in My Lai, Vietnam, the park was dedicated as a symbol of peace and forgiveness. Leaders of many countries, tourists, locals, and school groups visit the park and reflect on peace and harmony.

In 2001 the two countries entered the U.S.–Vietnam Bilateral Trade Agreement. Trade between the two nations has brought the countries closer together. Disputes regarding Vietnamese refugees, trade, and other issues are being discussed by both countries. Many Vietnamese Americans have traveled to Vietnam and have talked about and written about their experiences. Vietnam has also become a destination for other U.S. travelers who have interest in the country. These connections have helped to strengthen Vietnamese–U.S. relations.

FIND LINKS TO DISCOVER MORE ABOUT THE MANY WAYS THAT PEOPLE OF VIETNAMESE HERITAGE CONTRIBUTE TO LIFE IN AMERICA AT WWW.INAMERICABOOKS.COM.

FAMOUS VIETNAMESE AMERICANS

TONY BUI (b. 1973) Bui is a successful screenwriter and director.

Born in Saigon and only two years old when his family fled Vietnam, Bui grew up in California. There, his father ran a video rental store. Tony and his older brother, Timothy, watched thousands of free movies in their youth. They developed an early interest in filmmaking. Bui completed his first award–winning short film, *Yellow Lotus*, in 1995. He then went to work on *Three Seasons*. In 1999 that film won the Sundance Festival awards for best picture and best cinematography and the Audience Award. Bui's first two films were shot in Vietnam, a country he fell in love with as an adult. In 2001 Tony and Timothy released another movie, *Green Dragon*. *Green Dragon* tells about the camps that housed Vietnamese refugees in the United States in the 1970s.

VIET DINH (b. 1968) Dinh was born in Saigon and came to the United States as a refugee in 1978. He and his family spent a harrowing twelve days at sea in escaping Vietnam. As a young person, Dinh lived in Portland, Oregon, and in Fullerton, California. After working as a professor at Georgetown University Law Center, he served as clerk to various judges, including U.S. Supreme Court justice Sandra Day O'Connor. He has also worked as special counsel to various U.S. senators. In 2001 he became assistant attorney general for the Office of Legal Policy in Washington, D.C.

DANNY GRAVES (b. 1973) Born in Saigon, Graves is a pitcher for Major League Baseball's Cincinnati Reds. The hard–throwing right–hander attended the University of

Miami. Drafted by the Cleveland Indians, Graves made his debut for that team in 1996. Graves was traded to the Reds in 1997, where he has enjoyed great success as a late–inning

relief pitcher. In 2000 Graves made his first National League All–Star Game. He notched his one hundredth save and experienced his first games as a starting pitcher in 2002.

ANDREW LAM (b. 1964) Lam is a

journalist and writer who came to the United States from Saigon, Vietnam, at the age of eleven. He is an associate editor for the Pacific News Service and a regular commentator on National Public Radio. His short stories have appeared in *Transfer Magazine*, the *Vietnam Review*, and *Zyzzyva* and in the books *Watermark, Vietnam: A Traveler's Literary Companion*, and *Sudden Fiction (Continued)*. Lam served as a John S. Knight Fellow at Stanford University. He has won numerous awards, including the Society of Professional Journalists Outstanding Young Journalist Award and the World Affairs Council's Excellence in International Journalism Award.

DAT NGUYEN (b. 1975) Nguyen became the first Vietnamese American player in the National Football League after being drafted by the Dallas Cowboys in 1999. By his second season, he was the Cowboys' starting middle linebacker, despite being a bit smaller than most linebackers. Before being drafted by the Cowboys, he played at Texas A&M University. There he won the Lombardi Award for being the nation's top linebacker. In 1998 he also won the Bednarik Award as the top college defensive player. Nguyen works with several charities and was named to the American Football Coaches Association (AFCA) Good Works Team for community service and volunteer work. He grew up in Fulton, Texas, the son of Vietnamese refugees.

DUSTIN NGUYEN (b. 1962) Nguyen was born Nguyen Xuan Tri in Saigon, Vietnam, in 1962. His parents were both wealthy actors and outspoken opponents of Communism. The family fled Vietnam in the first wave of refugees and settled in St. Louis, Missouri. As a teenager, Dustin concentrated on learning English and studying martial arts. After high

school, he went to California. He became an actor, winning roles on television shows such as *Magnum, P.I.; General Hospital;* and *The A-Team.* In 1986 he received a starring role on *21 Jump Street.* Since then, Nguyen has appeared on numerous television shows, including *V.I.P.,* and in several movies. He also raises money and speaks for antidrug and antigang organizations.

JACQUELINE H. NGUYEN (b. 1965) Until 2002 Nguyen worked in  California as a prosecutor training assistant U.S. attorneys. Since then she has served as a federal judge on the Los Angeles Superior Court. Nguyen was born in Dalat, Vietnam. Her father was an officer in the South Vietnam army. When Nguyen was ten years old in 1975, her family fled and spent a brief period of time at Camp Pendleton, California. She and her family settled in California, where she has lived ever since.

KIEN NGUYEN (b. 1967) Nguyen, author of the memoir *The Unwanted* and the novel *The Tapestries,* is probably the best known Vietnamese American writer. Nguyen lived his early years in a Saigon mansion. He lived with his American father and his mother, who was from a wealthy family that worked for the last Vietnamese emperor. Trying to escape in 1975, he and his family watched a rescue helicopter explode over their heads from the rooftop of the U.S. embassy. Three years later, they tried to escape again. Nguyen finally left Vietnam in 1985 through the United Nations Orderly Departure Program. After spending time at a refugee camp in the Philippines, he arrived in the United States. With help from a benefactor in New York City, the penniless refugee went to dentistry school and opened his own practice. Nguyen works as a dentist one day a week, volunteering his services to help poor children.

QUYNH NGUYEN (b. 1976) Nguyen is a classical concert pianist living in New York City. Born in Hanoi, Vietnam, she began studying piano at the Hanoi Music Conservatory in Vietnam at age six and at age thirteen

won a scholarship competition to study at the Gnessin Institute in Moscow, Russia. She received her bachelor's degree at the Juilliard School and her master's degree at the Mannes College of Music and went on to enroll in the Doctor of Musical Arts program at the Graduate School of the City University of New York. She has performed concerts across the country and around the world and has won numerous awards, including the Artists International Presentation Award in 2000. Quynh Nguyen was one of the selected "19 young stars of tomorrow" in an article called "Young Artists: The Thrill of Discovery" in the Musical America 2004 edition, an international directory of performing arts. Nguyen is regularly featured on radio and television.

SHAYLA (b. 1975) Shayla Chau Dinh was born in Saigon, Vietnam, into a family of musicians. Her family fled to the United States in  1978 and settled in Houston, Texas, when Shayla (who goes only by her first name) was only a baby. She began to develop her singing talents

as a teenager and later began writing her own music. Her albums include *Open Up Your Heart, Funktify, Days and Nights of Missing You,* and *Dance Music.*

TUAN VO-DINH (b. 1948) Born in Vietnam, Vo-Dinh went to Switzerland at the age of seventeen to study physics and biophysical chemistry. He moved to the United States in 1975. He has since invented numerous devices that have  had a profound impact on health care. His inventions include a badge that records a worker's exposure to toxic chemicals. Other inventions include detection systems to locate damaged DNA, diabetes, and cancer. His technology is used in research centers and health-care facilities around the country.

TIMELINE

200s B.C.	Viets settle in the region that would later become Vietnam.
111 B.C. **A.D. 939**	China rules over the region that would later become Vietnam.
1535	The Portuguese enter the Vietnamese region.
1883	French colonial forces conquer Vietnam.
1939–1945	World War II is fought. Japanese forces take over Southeast Asia. At war's end, Vietnam declares independence.
1954	After eight years of French resistance to Vietnam's independence, a treaty results in the division of Vietnam. Violence between the north and south continues.
1956	The Vietnam War begins between North Vietnam and South Vietnam.
1964	The U.S. enters the Vietnam War, sending ground troops to aid South Vietnam.
1973	The U.S. military withdraws from the war.
1975	South Vietnam falls to North Vietnamese forces, and Vietnam is reunited under a Communist government. Refugees begin to flee the country.
1975–1980s	Vietnamese boat people leave the country via the sea.
1995	My Lai Peace Park is dedicated in My Lai, Vietnam.
2001	Vietnam and the United States sign the U.S.–Vietnam Bilateral Trade Agreement.
2003	Major exports to the United States from Vietnam increase 240% from 2002.

| web enhanced at **www.inamericabooks.com**

GLOSSARY

COMMUNIST: a person who believes in Communism. Communism is a social system in which property and goods are owned in common. In this system, a single party rules the state and controls the production of goods and services.

DELTA: an area around the mouth of a river where flooding deposits sediment and other nutrients, creating rich soil

DIALECT: a regional variety of a language

ETHNIC GROUP: a group of people sharing a common language, a common culture, and a common ancestry

EVACUATE: to remove people from a war zone or other dangerous area

GUERRILLA: fighting characterized by surprise attacks of small units on people and places. Guerrilla fighters often do not have a commanding officer, and their aim is to do as march harm to the enemy as possible without being caught.

MISSIONARY: a person on a religious mission, generally to promote a particular type of religion

REFUGEE: a person who flees to a foreign country for safety

REFUGEE CAMP: a place where refugees wait before going to the United States or another country. Second-wave Vietnamese refugees (the boat people) lived in such camps.

RELOCATION CENTER: a place where refugees waited before settling in the United States. The term generally applies to the centers where first-wave Vietnamese refugees waited.

TREATY: an agreement between two or more nations. The rules of a peace treaty outline how the different players in the struggle must act and what they must do to achieve peace.

Things to See and Do

HIGHGROUND VETERANS MEMORIAL, NEILLSVILLE, WISCONSIN

<http://www.thehighground.org/>

Highground was the inspiration for the My Lai Peace Park in Vietnam.

LITTLE SAIGON, WESTMINSTER, CALIFORNIA

<http://www.beachcalifornia.com/saigon.html>

Little Saigon is one of the largest and most prominent Vietnamese American communities in the United States. Clothing, foods, and other goods and services can be found in this large ethnic neighborhood.

MAM NON, ANN ARBOR, MICHIGAN

<http://www.mamnon.org/events/>

This group organizes activities throughout the year for families with children adopted from Vietnam. Some of the events for which they host celebrations are Tet, Tet Trung Thu (summer harvest), and Mam Non Day (a day to celebrate both Tet and to bring together families who are adopting Vietnamese children). Mam Non means "sprout" in Vietnamese.

TET

<http://www.tetinseattle.com/>

Tet is the celebration marking the Vietnamese Lunar New Year, which falls in January or February. Festivals are held in several major cities, including Seattle, Los Angeles, Chicago, and Dallas. Festivals include food, games, rides, parades, and more.

VIETNAM VETERANS MEMORIAL, WASHINGTON, D.C.

<http://www.nps.gov/vive/>

This memorial was built in 1982 to honor all the American people who died in the Vietnam War.

SOURCE NOTES

12 P. J. O'Rourke, *All the Trouble in the World: The Lighter Side of Overpopulation, Famine, Ecological Disaster, Ethnic Hatred, Plague, and Poverty* (New York: Atlantic Monthly Press, 1995), 327.

16 Jeremy Black, *European Warfare 1815–2000.* (New York: Palgrave Macmillan, 2002), 171.

19 "Timeline," *Vietnam Veterans Memorial of Greater Rochester, Inc.*, August 17, 2002, <http://www.vietnammemorial.org/grvvm1/virtual_tour/vt_timeline/timeline_03.htm> (January 15, 2004).

20 Phong Trieu, "The School on the Front Line," in *Between Two Fires* (New York: Praeger Publishers, 1970), 49.

24 Vo Phien, "The Key," in *The Other Side of Heaven: Postwar Fiction by Vietnamese and American Writers* (Willimantic, CT: Curbstone Press, 1995), 252.

31 Kien Nguyen, *The Unwanted* (New York: Back Bay Books, 2002), 220.

36 Troung Nhu Tang, *A Viet Cong Memoir* (New York: Random House, 1986), 293.

43 Hoaithi P. Nguyen, "Dialog Re: Vietnam Stories Since the War," *P.O.V.*, n.d., <http://www.pbs.org/pov/stories/vietnam/stories5/displaced.html> (January 15, 2004).

45 James M. Freeman, *Hearts of Sorrow: Vietnamese-American Lives* (Palo Alto, CA: Stanford University Press, 1991), 10.

50 W. D. Ehrhart, *My Lai Peace Park Project*, n.d., <http://www.mylaipeacepark.org/> (January 15, 2004).

SELECTED BIBLIOGRAPHY

Central Intelligence Agency. "Vietnam." *The World Factbook 2002*.<http://www.cia.gov/cia/publications/factbook/> (March 08, 2004). This document includes information on Vietnam's geography, people, government, economy, and history.

DeBonis, Steven. *Children of the Enemy: Oral Histories of Vietnamese Amerasians and Their Mothers*. Jefferson, NC: McFarland & Company, 1994. These oral histories were transcribed from recordings made at a refugee processing center in the Philippines.

Jamieson, Neil L. *Understanding Vietnam*. Berkeley: University of California Press, 1995. This book gives an excellent overview of the Vietnam War.

Karnow, Stanley. *Vietnam: A History*. New York: Penguin USA, 1997. This enormous book tells in detail the history of the country of Vietnam.

Levy, Debbie. *The Vietnam War*. Minneapolis: Lerner Publications Company, 2004. Learn about the causes and effects of the conflict that forced hundreds of thousands of Vietnamese people to flee their native land.

Lonely Planet. "Vietnam." *Worldguide*. 2003. <http://www.lonelyplanet.com/destinations/south_east_asia/vietnam/> (March 09, 2004). This publication offers information about the country of Vietnam, including holidays, climate, money, attractions, activities, environment, and history.

Saito, Lynne Tsuboi. *Ethnic Identity and Motivation: Socio-Cultural Factors in the Educational Achievement of Vietnamese American Students*. New York: LFB Scholarly Publishing LLC, 2002. This book examines the success of and problems faced by Vietnamese American students in high schools across the country.

Vietnam National Administration of Tourism. *Vietnam Tourism*. n.d. <http://www.vietnamtourism.com/update_info/e_index.asp> (March 09, 2004). This document provides data about the country's regions, history, people, and customs.

Further Reading & Websites

Nonfiction

Denenberg, Barry. *Voices from Vietnam.* New York: Scholastic, 1997. This book is a collection of letters, personal accounts, and narratives of journalists, citizens, diplomats, doctors, Vietnamese officials and soldiers, and others involved in the Vietnam War.

Galt, Margot Fortunato. *Stop This War! American Protest of the Conflict in Vietnam.* Minneapolis: Lerner Publications Company, 2000. Learn about the reaction in the United States to the Vietnam War during the 1960s and 1970s.

Greenberg, Keith, and John Isaac. *Vietnam: The Boat People Search for a Home.* New York: Blackbirch Marketing, 1996. This book is a photo essay about Vietnam's boat people.

Huynh, Quang Nhuong. *The Land I Lost: Adventures of a Boy in Vietnam.* New York: Harper Trophy, 1986. ———. *Water Buffalo Days: Growing Up in Vietnam.* New York: Harper Trophy, 1999. These two books are autobiographies relating the author's experiences growing up in Vietnam before coming to the United States.

Myers, Walter Dean. *A Place Called Heartbreak: A Story of Vietnam.* New York: Raintree/Steck–Vaughn, 1996. This is an account of U.S. servicemen in the Vietnam War. The book tells about the experiences of prisoners of war.

Nguyen, Chi, and Judy Monroe. *Cooking the Vietnamese Way.* Minneapolis: Lerner Publications Company, 2002. Learn more about Vietnamese cooking and culture, including traditional dishes and festival foods.

Springstubb, Tricia. *The Vietnamese Americans.* San Diego: Lucent Books, 2001. This book described the obstacles and achievements of many Vietnamese who left their homeland to settle in the United States.

Taus–Bolstad, Stacy. *Vietnam in Pictures.* Minneapolis: Lerner Publications Company, 2003. This book is an overview of the geography, history, culture, and economy of Vietnam.

Uschan, Michael V. *The Fall of Saigon: The End of the Vietnam War.* Portsmouth, NH: Heinemann Library, 2002. The book is an account of the final days of the Vietnam War.

Young, Marilyn Blatt, John J. Fitzgerald, and A. Tom Grunfeld. *Vietnam War: A History in Documents.* London: Oxford University Press Children's Books, 2002. Primary sources of information on the Vietnam War are collected in this volume.

FICTION

Boyd, Candy Dawson. *Charlie Pippin.* New York: Puffin, 1988. This is the story of a Vietnamese American girl trying to find out about her family's past in Vietnam.

Garland, Sherry. *Shadow of the Dragon.* New York: Harcourt Brace, 1993. In this novel, Danny Vo is the son of Vietnamese immigrants who have settled in Houston. He struggles with his desire to fit into American culture while remaining respectful of his family's cultural heritage.

Gibbons, Alan. *The Jaws of the Dragon.* Minneapolis: Lerner Publications Company, 1994. This is the story of a boy growing up in Vietnam.

Nelson, Theresa. *And One for All.* New York: Yearling Books, 1991. This is a fictional account of Vietnamese American young people trying to sort out their identities.

Surat, Michele Maria. *Angel Child, Dragon Child.* New York: Scholastic, 1989. Ut, a Vietnamese girl attending school in the United States, is lonely for her mother left behind in Vietnam. She seeks to find a way to bring her mother to the United States too.

Tran, Barbara, et. al, eds. *Watermark: Vietnamese American Poetry and Prose.* Philadelphia: Temple University Press, 1998. This compilation of short stories and poetry includes an Andrew Lam story that describes the introduction of a Vietnamese refugee boy into an eighth-grade American class.

Whelan, Glori. *Goodbye, Vietnam.* New York: Knopf, 1992. This story tells of a Vietnamese family escaping their homeland and eventually getting to America.

WEBSITES

INAMERICABOOKS.COM
<http://www.inamericabooks.com>
Visit www.inamericabooks.com,
the on-line home of the In America
series, to get linked to all sorts of
useful information. You'll find
historical and cultural websites
related to individual groups as well
as general information on
genealogy, creating your own
family tree, and the history of
immigration in America.

MAM NON
<http://www.mamnon.org/>
The site is devoted to sharing
Vietnamese culture among people
in the adoption community in the
United States.

THINGS ASIAN: EXPLORE THE
CULTURES OF ASIA
<http://www.thingsasian.com/>
This site offers stories, photos,
travel information, and more about
Asian cultures, including Vietnam.

VIETNAMESE BOAT PEOPLE
CONNECTION
<http://www.boatpeople.org>
This site isn't only about war-era
refugees, it's also about Vietnamese
American immigrants adapting to a

new land and culture while trying
to hold on to their own culture.
You can also read about Vietnamese
folk tales, cultural traditions,
heroes and heroines, as well as
individual refugee histories.
Content is in both English and
Vietnamese.

VN PLANET
<http://www.vnplanet.com/>
This is a cool portal about
Vietnamese around the world,
with pages for kids.

INDEX

ACKNOWLEDGMENTS: THE PHOTOGRAPHS IN THIS BOOK ARE REPRODUCED WITH THE PERMISSION OF: © Digital Vision, pp. 1, 3, 22; Courtesy of Geoff Hansen, p. 5; © Royalty-Free/CORBIS, p. 6; © R. Ramlochand/IDRC, p. 7; © Owen Franken/CORBIS, pp. 8, 54; © Leonard de Selva/CORBIS, p. 13; National Archives, p. 14; © CORBIS, p. 16; © Bettmann/CORBIS, pp. 17, 18, 20, 35; © Myron Dubee, Herald-Examiner Collection/Los Angeles Public Library, p. 21; Independent Picture Service, p. 25; © R. Charbonneau/IDRC, p. 27; © Ted Streshinsky/CORBIS, p. 28; © John Keenan, p. 29; © Nik Wheeler/CORBIS, p. 30; © UNHCR/V. Leduc, p. 31; © UNHCR/11217/J. M. Micaud, p. 32; © Howard Davies/CORBIS, p. 36; © Tim Page/CORBIS, pp. 37, 39; © MRS/US Catholic Conference, p. 38; © Steven Gold, Shades of L.A. Archives/Los Angeles Public Library, pp. 41, 47; © Dean Wong/CORBIS, p. 42; © Joseph Sohm; ChromoSohm Inc./CORBIS, p. 46; © Catherine Karnow/CORBIS, p. 48; © John Henley/CORBIS, p. 49; © Dean Musgrove, Herald-Examiner Collection/Los Angeles Public Library, p. 50; © Robert S. Halvey, p. 51; © David Butow/CORBIS SABA, p. 52; © Highground Vietnam Veterans Memorial, p. 56; © Robert Eric/CORBIS SYGMA, p. 58 (left); © Reuters NewMedia Inc./CORBIS, p. 58 (right); Courtesy Andrew Lam, p. 59 (left); © Pace Gregory/CORBIS SYGMA, p. 59 (right); © 2003, AsianWeek. Original publishing date 2003. Reprinted with permission, p. 60 (left); Courtesy Quynh Nguyen, p. 60 (right); Courtesy Shayla, p. 61 (left); Courtesy Tuan Vo-Dinh, p. 61 (right); Maps by Bill Hauser, pp. 15, 44.

Cover photography by: AP/Wide World Photos (top); © Royalty-Free/CORBIS (bottom); © Digital Vision (title, back cover).